God:
He is
My Flame
To Fame

A BOOK OF REFLECTIONS

Ikesia Nunez

authorHOUSE®

AuthorHouse™
1663 Liberty Drive
Bloomington, IN 47403
www.authorhouse.com
Phone: 1 (800) 839-8640

Published by AuthorHouse 12/28/2018

ISBN: 978-1-5462-7395-0 (sc)
ISBN: 978-1-5462-7431-5 (e)

Library of Congress Control Number: 2018915255

Dedication

I would like to dedicate this book of reflections to my Heavenly Father, in the name of Jesus Christ. It was through his strength and guidance that all of this became possible. Even through all the sleepless nights and being exiled by many, tormented and disregarded by those whom I cherished but who did not see me as the diamond that God has created me to be, he remained by my side, whispering to me that I am not alone, and he is not finished with me. He had to get me through all the dirt so that I could shine in spite my past.

I could go on and on about all the things my great and gracious God has brought me through. Instead, I am going to praise and worship him because he has redeemed, restored, fixed, molded, and prepared me for the front lines of battle. He is my flame to fame. No matter how hard a project may be, he continues to lead, guide, and direct me down all the safe passageways. No one could fathom how he could take a hurt, misled, and underappreciated soul and turn it into a masterpiece. That's why he is the source of the joy that sustains me in this lifetime. I lift my hands up to him and proclaim, "You deserve it all." I know he will be with me through this journey and all other journeys to come.

Who Is Christ, and What Is His Purpose?

Where do we begin on this subject? I would say that Christ is the reason for our being. The reason I say this is that without him, we would not have salvation from condemnation of our sins. He is grace given by God to free us from the bondage that holds us back from the world.

First, let's explain what the grace of God means. Grace is the unmerited mercy (favor) God gave to humankind by sending his Son to die on a cross; this delivers eternal salvation. What is salvation? Salvation is deliverance from sin and its consequences. What is unmerited mercy? It is undeserved compassion or forgiveness shown toward someone who is within one's power to discipline.

Now that we have an understanding of God's grace, we can understand that Jesus is a gift to us from God so that we may be at peace and have faith and hope. Luke 2:10-11 says, "I bring to you news that will bring great joy to the people. The Savior, yes, The Messiah, The Lord Has been born today in Bethlehem." This scripture says that our promised deliverer, the one who will save us from danger and has authority over us, has been born unto us and will bring us great joy. Notice it doesn't mention great happiness, because this trait resembles your feelings about how the circumstance affects your emotion; it's a fleshly or worldly trait. As for joy, no matter what occurs in your life, you will remain at peace because you know you are not alone in any situation; Jesus will fight your battles.

Therefore, we must confess and believe that Jesus is our Lord and Savior. He is the one who will intercede for us to break away from chains that constantly hold us back, such as guilt, pain, past hurts, faults, self-loathing, and so forth—all the things that prevent us from moving forward towards what God has planned for us. Unless we invite Jesus into our lives, He cannot break these chains. He is the mediator between us and God. He sits beside God as an intermediary, giving us partnership with him. John 14:6 says, "Jesus is the way, the life and the truth; no one gets to the Father except through the Son." This means that Jesus is the only way that we can have communion with God. He will work within us to break all our sinful natures so that we will begin to form a relationship with God.

When we are born, we go through developmental stages. First, we babble and coo, and then we say our first words (most likely, "Daddy"). As we grow, our vocabulary grows. That's how our Christian walk grows. First, we must confess Christ as our Lord and Savior. As he continues to minister and work within us, we become closer and closer to understanding him and our behavior begins to resemble his throughout our lives. After this relationship develops, we become closer to God, forming a relationship with him while Christ is with us.

To sum it up, you must accept Jesus into your life so that he can save you from this world. Luke 19:10 says, "For the Son of Man came to seek and save those who are lost." We are all lost in this world, allowing it to take us over. But once we accept the invitation of Jesus Christ, we no longer seek this world. We begin to seek salvation and enjoy this life no matter what.

God's grace and peace be upon you all, and may you continue to stay on the vine of Christ, so you can grow closer to him. "Yes, I am the vine; you are the branches. Those who remain in me, and I in them, will produce much fruit. For apart from me you can do nothing" (John 15:5). To learn more about Jesus Christ, read the book of John, and allow God to give you the revelations that are for you. Until next time, stay blessed and full of faith.

Relationship with God

Have you ever felt like you are distant from God? I have felt this way on many occasions, not because I wanted to but because I didn't know what it meant to have a relationship with him. *Relationship* means being connected with someone or something. I would always cry out, "Lord, help me," when things became unbearable. But I didn't feel as though he heard or cared for me. Once I shouted those words, I would begin to cry, really not understanding that either.

Then one day, my sister-in-law explained how being connected with God gives you peace in all situations, no matter how big or small. She encouraged me to read the Bible and get connected with a church. That sounded crazy to me. As a child, I went to church but really didn't get anything out of it. However, I began to go to church, and the more I went, the more I engaged in reading and understanding the Bible. I started to understand how God was the creator of all, and how he knew me before my parents did. Psalm 139:13 says, "For You did form my inward parts; You did knit me together in my mother's womb." This means he intricately created me in his image.

I noticed that once I accepted Christ into my life, he began breaking all my bondages. I was no longer condemned by my faults. I had been forgiven, and a new slate was given to me. This opened the pathway for me to communicate with God. Scripture says, "We are made right with God by placing our faith in Jesus Christ" (Romans 3:22). This means that for us to be able to understand the love of God, we must first accept his Son, who intercedes on our behalf. I began to open my heart more to him through prayer and by talking to him about everything. I noticed I couldn't go a day without praising and worshipping him.

My life began to come together. Things that used to bother me didn't bother me so much. I was able to release my burdens to him and really feel unexplainable peace. It was like everything was lifted off my shoulders, and I believed and had faith that everything was going to be okay.

Now I see what it means to have a relationship with him. He took away my pains and sorrows, giving me refuge from them all. Even through suffering, I know God will never leave or forsake me because for me to receive all he has planned for me, I must endure the hardships to reap his righteous harvest. Scripture says, "After you have suffered awhile, He will restore, support, strengthen you and He will place you on a firm foundation" (1 Peter 5:10). This simply means that through suffering, God builds you in ways only he can. The more the communication lines between us remain active, the more life can be maintained. We just have to know, believe, and have hope and faith in him no matter what. This allows him to lead us on our journeys through life.

Father, Son, and Holy Spirit

When I say these words, they bring sweet joy to my soul. They may be short in length, but they make grand outcomes in our lives. The Father created us in his image, the Son saved us from condemnation of our sins and bondages, and the Holy Spirit redeemed us, so we can live with Christ in us. Genesis 1:27 says, "So God created man in His own image, in the image and likeness of God He created him; male and female He created them." This tells us we are creations of our Father—God—who made us all according to his will. When we think about this, we realize how great it is to be made in the image of the Father. He controls every attribute given to us, so we know we are his masterpieces. We know God not only created us but loves us so much that nothing can separate his love from us. Romans 8:39 says, "Nor height, nor depth, nor anything else in all creation will be able to separate us from the love of God which is Christ Jesus our Lord."

This brings us to the Son, whom God sent down upon this earth to give us salvation, peace, love, hope, and faith. Isaiah 9:6 says, "For to us a Child is born, to us a Son is given; and the government shall be upon His shoulder, and His name shall be called Wonderful Counselor, Mighty God, Prince of Peace." Through the death of Christ, the Holy Spirit descended from heaven to advocate for us through Christ. This is the spirit that lives in us; it directs us in communicating with the Father. John 14:26 says, "But when the Father sends the Advocate as my representative—that is the Holy Spirit—He will teach you everything and will remind you of everything I have told you." See, the three go hand in hand; you cannot have one without the others. Through understanding and the significance of the three, I was able to defeat many trials in my life. I just had to keep faith as my foundation and allow the intercession of Christ to take over my soul.

The Significance of Prayer

Don't worry about anything; pray about everything.
Tell God what you need, thank him for all He has done.
Then you will experience God's peace, which exceeds
anything we can understand. His peace will guard
your hearts and minds as you live in Christ Jesus.
—Philippians 4:6–7

This scripture passage really expresses the importance of taking all your cares to God. When you pray, it is a relationship between you and your Abba (God). It's considered a relationship because when you pray, it's an intimate conversation just between the two of you. Here is where you lay it all out. You express your innermost feelings, frustrations, guilt, and anything else you may feel uncomfortable speaking about with others because you feel ashamed, judged, or even condemned. This is the place where there will be none of that; all it will be is refreshing. It is refreshing, because once you release anything to God, as far as the east is from the west, he does not remember your transgressions, faults, or disappointments. All he does is forgive and renew you with his constant love and grace.

A lot of us tend to call a friend or become angry when life takes unexpected turns, before we bring it to the throne. The reason we do this is that we, following our human nature, always turn to others before our Lord. We get angry and bitter with him when the decisions we make don't go according to our plans. Now, we must understand, how can God intercept or intervene in our issues if we don't invite him to guide us before catastrophe takes place. We must seek God with all our hearts above all things (Matthew 6:33). That is when you will feel his constant peace and discipline.

To understand God's discipline read Hebrews 12. The first and foremost thing is that we must accept his Son, Jesus Christ. The reason this is a crucial step in your communion with God is that Jesus is the intermediate guide who binds us with God. This means that to get to the Father, we must go through the Son. We must accept Jesus, so he can intercede to break away all these earthly things that infect us and keep a wedge between us and God. To fully understand Jesus Christ and his reasoning, read Hebrews 8–10. Always remember, for our lives to flourish, we must constantly seek God through prayer and always remember how faithful he is to us.

P—Praise and thank God.

R—Repent and surrender all to him.

A—Ask God what you need (invite him into your life).

Y—Yield and let God have the right of way in all situations.

To sum it all up, prayer trumps anxiety, frustration, disappointment, and so on. All we must do is surrender and give ourselves fully to Jesus Christ first; then we will be partnered with God. To learn more about this, read 1 Corinthians 1.

I hope this is beneficial to you in your spiritual walk.

Stay blessed and always pray no matter what; keep the communication lines open between you and God; stay on the vine of Christ to flourish (John 15:5).

Choices and Decisions

Many things in life cause us to make different choices. When I say this, I am simply stating that God gives us his wisdom, knowledge, comprehension, discernment, and understanding each day, which directs our actions, choices, and decisions. Proverbs 2:6 says, "For the Lord grants wisdom; from his mouth comes knowledge and understanding." He gives us wisdom, and in turn we must choose or decide on our own as he directs us through Christ. He has created us to be able to think according to his will. The only way we can differentiate between God's will and ours is through the intermediator, Christ. We must allow Christ to work within us, so he can direct us each step of the way. He cleanses us from the inside out, which allows us to become more and more like him.

Often, we make sudden choices or decisions according to our emotional state, and they're reflected in momentary actions. I say this because whenever you make choices or decisions in a second or in an emotional moment, they do not benefit you in the long run; it's just for that second to ease whatever is hurting or bothering you. It's intended as a quick fix, but God does not quick fix; he restores, rebuilds, strengthens, and renews all things for our betterment.

Now that the introduction was given to you, let's distinguish between choices and decisions. Choices are for the now, and decisions have longevity. For example, I chose to ride the school bus each morning. In turn I decided to get my license, so I wouldn't have to ride the bus. See, when we make a choice, it's just something that helps us at that moment, but when we make a decision, it continues to grow us on a continuous basis. Following Christ is a decision because he continues to enhance you every day of your life. We must make it a decision to get right with God and have a relationship with him through Christ, because he is the one who continues to shield and protect us from the clutches of the evil one. We cannot handle this life without daily encouragement from the words of God, which will never change.

Isaiah 40:6-8 says, "People are like grass, and their beauty is like flowers. The grass withers and flowers fade, but the words of the Lord stand forever." Simply saying, nothing on earth is constant, but putting your hope in the words of God will maintain you because his words are forever, without changing or conforming to the ways of this world.

To conclude, let's not allow moments of frustration, guilt, hurt, our thoughts, or our emotions make our decisions or choices.

Let's have a still mind focused on Christ, which will help us make the appropriate decisions and choices in our life. Give yourself to Christ so he can work through you; he will break all chains or bondages that are holding on to you. Let's keep our minds on all the things up above, not on the earthly things (Colossians 3:2). I will leave you with this scripture, Proverbs 4:23, "Be careful what you think because your thoughts run your life." Be diligent in focusing on the faithfulness, greatness, and sovereignty of God because he is always present through it all.

In life, we go through many trials and tribulations that test our strength, faith, hope, and belief. However, we have been given grace through it all. Grace is the undeserved favor that God has given us because he so loves us as his children. He says in Ephesians that we were foreordained to be adopted through Christ into his family. The more we fixate on the circumstances instead of the glory of our God, through Christ, we become bitter, angry, even unforgiving, because we are focused on whatever is causing the pain. We do not feel or see that God is working things out for our good. As humans, we expect changes to occur quickly, according to our will and strength; however, God's will and strength are much bigger and better than ours because he is strengthening us for the long haul, not just for the moment.

If we will just allow Christ into our heart, mind, body, and soul, he will do wonders for us. When I say this, I mean that he will begin to intercede in us to break through all the condemnation, bondage, and chains that are holding us back from having joy in our lives. Matthew 11:28 states, "Come to me all who are weary and carry heavy burden, for I will give you rest." We have no rest because we are carrying all our burdens. We were not made to carry these burdens; rather we were made to give them to our Father, in the name of Jesus. That's why Jesus died on Calvary for us—so we would not have to bear these burdens. Below, you will find scriptures that will help you seek God, in the name of Jesus, through all circumstances, instead of doing things on your own. Our way is not working. We are still stuck in the circle of torment because of our own negligence.

Psalm 23:1—"The Lord is my shepherd, I have all that I need."
Proverbs 3:5-6—"Trust in the Lord with all your heart. Do not depend on your own understanding. Seek his will in all you do, and he will show you which path to take."
Romans 12:12—"Rejoice in our confident hope. Be patient in times of trouble and keep praying."
Romans 12:1—"Do not copy the behavior and customs of this world, but let God transform you into a new person by changing the way you think."
Psalm 68:19—"Praise the Lord; praise God our savior! For each day he carries us in his arms."
Romans 5:3—"We can rejoice too, when we run into problems and trials, for we know that they help us develop endurance."
Exodus 14:14—"The Lord himself will fight for you; just stay calm."
Proverbs 21:2—"People may be right in their own eyes, but the Lord examines their heart."
Isaiah 12:2—"See, God has come to save me. I will trust in him and not be afraid."

Suffering

When we go through hard times, it can take a toll on our faith. When I say this, I'm simply saying that we become consumed with the opposition, replaying certain incidents in our minds over and over. We pray, but it just seems like it goes away at that moment and as time elapses, it comes back. This signifies that we are not allowing God to have full control over the situation. First, what does suffering mean? It describes the state of undergoing pain, distress, or hardship. Examples of suffering are financial difficulties, health issues, and loss.

Now, since we have identified the meaning and some examples of suffering, let's talk about ways we can defeat it. The only way we can defeat suffering is by letting ourselves be consumed by the words of God. This is the only real and potent remedy for suffering; it has proved to be true because he is the only one who can release us from the sufferings of this world. Many people can recite the scripture found in James that says resist the devil and he shall flee. However, we have forgotten the verse that comes before it, which says we should humble ourselves before God. The full verse says, "So humble yourselves before God. Resist the devil, and he will flee from you" (James 4:7).

When we humble ourselves, we are becoming submissive to God and giving him the power in our lives; we are no longer allowing our behavior to overpower us but his will. Therefore, once we submit and relinquish ourselves to him, we have the power to defeat the accuser. God has given us a weapon against the accuser, which is Jesus. One must know, believe in, and accept Jesus as his or her Lord and Savior, because he is the one who intercedes and breaks all chains, bondage, and condemnation from us. Romans 10:13 says, "For all who call on the name of the Lord will be saved."

We were not placed on this earth to be entangled in suffering but to enjoy this world regardless of the circumstances. Romans 5:3–4 says, "Not only so, but we also glory in our sufferings, because we know that sufferings produces perseverance; perseverance, character; and character, hope." This scripture is saying that through suffering, we continue to be steadfast in doing what is right despite the difficulty, because it produces in us a character of hope. When we persevere, we are moving forward regardless of the obstacles before us because we know there is hope in believing that God will never fail or abandon us; we can go on because we have faith. Going through suffering is hard only when we don't rely on God and know who holds the keys to our lives; everything that is given to us, whether good or bad, is orchestrated by God.

John 3:27 says, "No one can receive anything unless God gives it from heaven." We must maintain our belief and faith in God, Jesus, and the Holy Spirit, because the Trinity works constantly behind the scenes of everything to give us fulfillment in this life. Let's conquer suffering by allowing the Trinity to work within us to build a strong character of perseverance so we will not easily fall victim to the accuser's lies and deception.

In conclusion, let's not remain in insanity, which means continuously doing the same thing but expecting different results. Instead of having wavering faith in God, let's be steadfast in our thinking, constantly praying and seeking him through it all so we can grow stronger in our spirit. When our spirit grows, it weakens the flesh in which we are no longer tied to the world's deceptive behavior. "Greater is He that is within me than He that is in this world" (1 John 4:4).

To learn more about suffering, read the book of Job; it depicts how suffering can manifest and cause you to be overwhelmed with condemnation. However, through it all you will see how God remains the same and is constantly there, waiting to intervene and help you.

Discouraged

I want to ask a question: Have any of you ever suffered from being discouraged? Being discouraged means you have lost confidence in something. Many of us, myself included, have second-guessed God on many occasions. I say this because whenever a circumstance occurs, most of us try to figure it out on our own first. When our decision doesn't work, we pray as a last resort. Now, if we understand the obedience of God, we must seek him first in all things. Philippians 4:6–7 says, "Worry about nothing instead pray about everything; tell God what you need and thank Him for all He has done." When we pray to God about everything, no matter how big or small, that exemplifies a relationship with him. We are allowing him to be a part of our lives, in which he can intervene to point us in the right direction, which gives us the proper decisions in any matter.

If we would just seek him throughout, it would eliminate all the confusion and chaos that happens when we seek ourselves. This world in which we live in throws a lot of curveballs at us at any given time. However, if our trust and confidence is in God, he gives us refuge from it all. Psalm 62:8 says, "Trust in, lean on, rely on, and have confidence in Him at all times; pour out your hearts before Him. God is a refuge for us (a fortress and a high tower)." When we read this scripture, it is simply saying that we are heavily protected by God, and nothing can penetrate his protection for us. All we must do is be steadfast in our faith; he does everything else.

Now, you may be wondering how this can be when we do not see changes quickly and need things immediately. That is why faith means having complete trust or confidence in someone or something. 2 Corinthians 5:7 says, "We live by believing not seeing." When we believe and know that God is our source of life, nothing can defer our belief and hope in him. We can have this confidence only through Christ. He is the mediator between us and God. Just to give a little biblical background, God so loved the world that he gave his one and only son, Jesus, to die for us so we can be given free salvation, peace, hope, and faith without any condemnation; he was the sacrificial lamb for all our sins. John 14:6 says, "Jesus is the way, the life and the truth; no one gets to the father except through the Son." We must accept Jesus Christ as our Lord and Savior, so he can break all chains, bondages, and condemnation. Therefore, we can freely accept that God is our creator and holds the keys to our lives. To understand more about the reason for Christ, read the book of John; it is very informative.

To sum it all up, we must continue to place all our hope and belief in God, knowing that he will get us through anything we are going through, all according to his righteous will. Remember, it's his will, not ours. We must patiently wait on the Lord. God's time is the perfect time, whereas ours is always of the now. I'll wait on God, because I know his ways are for eternity (will last forever), whereas my ways are for the time being. God will help us through situations and give us options so that we don't have to continue to repeat the same mishaps. So, when you feel discouraged, pray to God for help, and he will release you from that captivity. Remember this scripture: "Don't be afraid, for I am with you; don't be discouraged for I am your God" (Isaiah 41:10).

God knows that we will have times of weakness. That is why we have to constantly rely on him. As your soul grows closer to God, you begin to acknowledge it more quickly when discouraging thoughts arrive. Pray and talk with the authority of God against them to release the tension and give it to God. First Peter 5:7 says, "Cast all your cares upon God because He cares for you." Just stay in constant contact with God. That is how we defeat discouraging thoughts. Stay blessed and focused on our creator, God, and continue to allow Christ's intercession within you.

Storms

When we are going through the storms of life, we must maintain our faith that God is always with us. He promised to never leave, forsake, or abandon us. Below you will find powerful scriptures that will help you through these storms. Do not allow your circumstances to overshadow continuous faithfulness in God.

Judges 6:12 says, "Mighty hero, the Lord is with you." Whenever the evil one starts to make you feel worthless, unloved, or any other emotion that takes away from the masterpiece you are, just say this scripture over and over. It will enhance your faith and the reality of knowing that you are loved, and nothing can separate you from the love of the Father.

Psalms 46:10 says, "Be still and know that I am God." Know that God is changing things in your favor; you must first allow his presence into your circumstances, in which he will make all things new, according to his will and power. When you are going through things, it just means that you are so loved that he has given you the opportunity to endure, which increases your faith in him.

Psalms 4:8 says, "In peace I lie down to sleep, for you alone, O Lord, will keep me safe." No matter how big or small things may be, God has you covered with his unfailing love, compassion, and favor. This prayer gives you peace through it all.

Controlling the Tongue

For if we could control our tongues, we would be perfect
and could control ourselves in every other way.

—James 3:2

As we read this scripture, it makes us think how vital our tongue really is. It can either build us up or destroy us. When you say uplifting words, causing others to grow, you are demonstrating the proper usage of the tongue and resembling Christ. However, when you belittle, judge, curse, and so on, you are using the tongue as the devil's rifle. This statement means that whenever you praise or use kind words, you are being an image of Christ, but when you use earthly words against others, you are doing what the devil likes, destroying one another. Anything that is kind and uplifting comes from heaven (Christ Jesus), and anything that devours or brings someone down is of this earth.

Read Galatians 5:22–23; l always go back to this scripture, because it is where you come to understand the fruits of the spirit and worldly traits. For the tongue to be controlled, we must constantly seek God's wisdom so that we are able to comprehend and use proper discretion. To do this, we must first understand wisdom, which is the ability to judge correctly and follow the best course of action, based on knowledge and understanding. This is what God gives his children. Wisdom comes from his mouth and enters our mind, causing a chain reaction of knowledge and understanding; this is where the discretion or judgment comes from.

To understand more about God's wisdom, read Proverbs 1. For example, take this scenario: You are driving, and someone cuts you off. Before thinking, you blurt out malice through curse words, calling the other driver everything except his God-given name. This is an example of how quickly emotions can take over your thought process. However, if you stop and listen for the small voice of God, he will give you the wisdom to relax and know there's no need to pursue an issue that's not worth it; you can pray for the other driver and continue with your day. This shows that we are emotionally driven, which causes us to lash out no matter how big or small the situation is. However, if we dismember the emotions and focus on God, no situation will cause us to act out of character.

This is all a part of guarding our hearts, because whatever goes in comes out. In other words, when offenses or hurts enter, all that exits through our tongue is viciousness because we feel hurt, threatened, or even disrespected. When we protect ourselves from offenses, we eliminate the outpours of anger and vulgar speech. In order to accomplish this, we must stay on the vine of Christ so that we will be able to conquer the constant attacks of the evil one. Remember this: Greater is He that is in me than He of this world. When Christ is in you, you continue to portray his characteristics. No situation will cause an uproar, because he will be there guiding you through it all. Read Proverbs 4 (about guarding the heart), John 15 (about the vine of Christ), and 1 John 4 (understanding that Christ is within you).

In conclusion, the only way we can control our tongues is to constantly seek God through reading his words of truth; this will help you stay focused and use proper judgment with him right beside you.

Hope

What does hope mean in one's life? Is it believing or having a feeling? Let's begin with the meaning of hope. It is a feeling of expectation and desire for a certain thing to happen. Now, when we read this, we learn that hope is a feeling and a desire for something to happen. That's what God wants us to have in regard to him when we are going through things.

I have been struggling these last couple of days, trying to wrap my mind around hope in the face of these constant giants that are arising in my life. I know that God is here with me through it all, but I battle with hope and understanding. God does things on his time, and we must patiently wait on him, which is much easier said than done. We are human, which means we have human tendencies. We want things to be handled now rather than wait. God knows that's a weakness, but when we call upon him to help us through our mishaps, he gives us strength to continue to go on even through the turbulence. Second Corinthians 12:9 says, "My power works best in weakness, so that the power of Christ can work through me." This is simply saying that when we are weak, God strengthens us through Christ. Christ continues to intercede within us to manifest the hope and faith in knowing that we will overcome this; all we must do is have a foundation built on God. Isaiah 40:31 says, "But those who trust in the Lord will find new strength."

To believe God's words, we must have hope in knowing that he will follow through with what he says. God has given me the opportunity to reflect on all his faithfulness that he has poured upon me. I realized that he has not brought me this far to leave me; he loves me too much for that, and I must be obedient to him. Obedience means being submissive to another's will. Therefore, it is God's will that we maintain our hope and faith in him, because he will never abandon or fail us. He loves us so much that he gave his one and only Son, that whoever believes in him shall not perish but have eternal life. I believe and know that God is handling everything in my life. He has plans and outcomes ready for me; all I have to do is continue to allow him to restore and rebuild me when he breaks me down to know he is God. I must not intervene but must accept and continue to follow his will for me. Hebrews 10:23 says, "Let us hold tightly without wavering to the hope we affirm, for God can be trusted to keep his promise."

How Faith in God Helped My Marriage

First let's continue to thank God, for he is forever faithful. When we go through tests and trials in our marriage, this is the time when we seek God, through Christ, for guidance and strategies to work through it all. Matthew 6:33 says, "Seek first His kingdom and righteousness and these things shall be given unto you." We seek him through prayers by the Holy Spirit in Jesus's name. By doing this, we begin to receive ways of handling all things in the appropriate manner.

In the Bible, the book of Exodus played a vital part in my marriage's growth. It spoke volumes about knowing that no matter how hard or difficult an obstacle may be in my mind, nothing can stand against what God has joined together, and his purpose will prevail in everything. In the next paragraphs, you will see how God's power and will for us will weaken anything or anyone who is against us.

The book of Exodus depicts the exile of the Israelites from Egypt, and God used Moses as the one to lead them. Moses was born an Israelite but was raised as an Egyptian. When he became a man, he was informed that he was in fact an Israelite; instead of being sheltered inside the palace, he chose to be outside with his people. To make a long story short, Moses killed an Egyptian, which caused him to flee and be in total seclusion for forty years. Now, this is how God is glorified: he spoke to Moses through a burning bush and told him that he would be the one to get his people out of enslavement. Moses couldn't understand why God chose him, but when God has a plan and purpose for you, not even you can block it. God knew Moses would question himself, and that's why he used Aaron, Moses's brother, to be a part of the puzzle as well. After many attempts, the Israelites were set free and went toward the Promised Land.

As for me, the Lord allowed me to read this over and over to understand that what's in front of me is to strengthen my marriage, not tear it apart, because he has not forgotten us. I was praying for God to change my situation, but actually God needed to change me. I was holding on to so many hurts and so much brokenness that I was shooting everyone down instead of helping them. I mean, I was a monster; I spoke to people without respect and love because I was harboring resentment about the things the person had done to me in the past.

Many times, I wanted to go, but I just couldn't leave the situation. I didn't understand why I couldn't leave, because it was not healthy for me. One day God pointed me to John 8:7, which says, "Let him who is without sin cast the first stone." It was like a light clicked on and the replay button started to show me how I was. I thought I was innocent in all of that, but I wasn't. I was just as vicious as the person who had hurt me. Neither one of us could see past each other's faults, which crippled our ability to grow closer. It was separating us. I began to pray for a clean and forgiving heart toward them, asking God to teach me to love with compassion instead of resentment. Because of my constant reliance on God, through Christ, he took me and began to give me a workout from the inside out. I started to reconnect more and more with his scriptures; as a result, my conversations were driven toward uplifting, love, and respect for others. He broke down those walls.

I understood when God said he gives us dominion over the serpents. I took back the authority from the serpent, which had weakened it. I am still being prepared and molded, but I now know that I fight my battles in prayer; this releases the force of God to take charge and beat all that is coming against me. The book of Proverbs says that a wise woman edifies her home. I began to lift up my household instead of beating it down. God has created us from the man's rib, and just as the rib is an important part of our anatomy, we are vital to our spouses. I have learned how to grab hold of the good qualities instead of focusing on everything that is wrong. As the scriptures tell us, look beneath the surface so you can judge correctly. Keep your faith in the Father, Son, and Holy

Words of Hope During Pain

During these times, we must pursue God every day. He is the only one who will ease our pain and give us rest through it all. Psalm 126:5 says, "They that sow in tears shall reap in joy." God is telling us that even through all our sorrows and tears, he will give us joy; all we must do is remain in the foundation of his love and compassion. Trust in God through it all; he loves you and will sustain you. Just know that all your steps are ordered by God, who is in control of it all; we must surrender it all and let him work through the pain and sorrow.

Pray and allow God into your life; give him the right to intervene on your behalf. May God continue to shower you with his compassion, tenderhearted mercies, love, full armor, wisdom (to understand and accept the unknown), discernment (to always follow his will), and favor. Stay blessed and joyous through it all. Lamentations 3:32 says, "Though he brings grief, he also shows compassion because of the greatness of his unfailing love." Rest in the comforting arms of God in the mighty name of Jesus Christ.

Unanswered Prayers

First let's always give thanks to our Heavenly Father for his faithfulness toward us, for his promises are our armor and protection. Sometimes when I pray, I feel lost and without substance. When I say this, I mean that I feel as though my prayers go into the openness of the air without return. I pray and pray about many things with no results. One could say that I am losing my faith in God, but that's not so. I'm just stuck in my own thoughts at the moment. I am trying to figure out things that were not meant for me to do. John 14:1 says "Don't let your hearts be troubled, trust in God." 1Peter 5:7 says, "Give all your worries and cares to God for he cares for you." My mind floats off in thin air because I am not focusing on the many promises that our gracious God has given us; instead, I am stuck trying to figure out or make sense of the things that are happening in my mind.

When we become trapped in our own thoughts, we disregard what's prominent, which is the sacrifice of Christ Jesus. When we really understand and absorb the brutality of what he endured for our freedom, there is nothing of this world that should make us feel lost or out of place. He took on all our sins and chains of this world so that we can live in peace through him. When God does not answer our prayers, that just means that he has other things that need to be worked out within us first. We know that God is almighty and will always take care of his children, because Romans 10:3 says, "Everyone who call on the name of the Lord will be saved."

For us to call on him, we must have a relationship with him through Christ because he is the way, the life, and the truth; no one gets to the Father except through the Son. We must give ourselves fully to Christ and continue to allow him to cleanse us from the inside out; we are constantly being prepared and molded in ways that only the Father can do through Christ. Focus more on the things of heaven instead of these earthly things.

God has promised to never leave, forsake, abandon, or fail us, and I trust in his every word because all of his promises are true, and he is trustworthy. May the grace of God keep you where the will of God takes you.

Forgiveness

Continued thanks to our Heavenly Father for all his faithfulness through Christ Jesus. Many of us struggle with forgiveness because it's the easiest thing that the evil one can use to keep us from progressing in the direction in which our Father wants us to go. When we hold on to the hurts that were inflicted on us by others, it makes us angry and disgruntled. We are unable to see past the hurt, which causes our hearts to harden against those who caused us pain. We are unable to see the positive in them because the hurt is so vivid in our hearts and minds, but in Luke 6:37, Jesus says, "Forgive others and you will be forgiven."

When we forgive others for their faults or mishaps that they have done to us, our love for them prospers. The scriptures tell us that love covers a multitude of sins and lack of forgiveness divides homes, marriages, friendships, and families, to name just a few. The evil one causes this division because he likes to separate; in contrast, God unites. In order for us to forgive, we must accept that we all have fallen short of the glory of God. That is why he has given us salvation through his Son, Jesus Christ, who paid the ultimate price for us all.

We must make a mental note of the forgiveness that Jesus had to give to all those who kicked, punched, whipped, mocked him, and hung him on the cross, so that all of mankind can be freed from the sins of this world. Before he died, in Luke 23:34, Jesus said, "Father, forgive them for they do not know what they are doing." Even through all his pain and suffering, Jesus still gave forgiveness to us all. He knew that because of his forgiveness, mankind has no guilt to be held over them from his crucifixion.

Jesus died for us to be free. Do not allow an outpouring of resentment to keep you from progressing in your family, marriage, and so on. Instead, give it all to God, through Christ, and allow him to ease the hurt and give you a clean and purified heart. Pray for a heart that forgives all those who have hurt you, and in turn, pray for those whom you have hurt to forgive you. Pray without ceasing and fix your mind on Christ. May the grace of God keep you where the will of God may take you.

Fasting

I first want to explain the meaning of fasting, which is abstinence from food or drink as an element of religious devotion. One may think that fasting is part of being religious, but to me, it's part of a relationship with God that helps you grow closer to him, through Christ. When I did my first fast, man, I mean I was angry and miserable. I just kept complaining and complaining. It just was not in the cards for me, but when God has a plan for your life, he will bring you to the real meaning and significance of fasting.

Well, didn't he show me who was in charge. All day my head was hurting without any relief, until God used a coworker to stop me in my tracks. She said, abruptly, "Stop your complaining. You do not have to be so disgruntled. If you don't want to do it, then do not do it—eat already." My eyes just lit up like those of a deer caught in the headlights. I went to my desk and just wandered off into space; then thirty minutes later it was time to go home. Do not forget, my head was still pounding as if someone had hit me full force with their fist. I got into my car. As I was driving, Danny Gokey song "Masterpiece" came on. My eyes started to tear up, and in the blink of an eye I was apologizing to my Heavenly Father for my attitude toward the fast. I reached out, shouting, "Please help me through this, help me get closer to you, through Christ." I was praying and seeking him the whole ride home. My headache began to subside.

I was going through all these motions because my flesh wanted the pleasures of this world and was weakening my willingness to go forward. I wanted desperately to eat or drink anything. That's why in Matthew 26:41, Jesus says, "For the spirit is willing but the flesh is weak." I was not allowing the Holy Spirit to strengthen me; instead I was working off my own strength. In the next paragraphs, I will explain how my strength in God, through Christ, made it possible for me to do the fast with peace and authority, knowing that I was covered by him, in the name of Jesus.

When we focus more on this world and what it gives, we begin to stray from God, because to us all our needs are met. However, unless we grow nearer to God through constant communication, knowing and understanding his ways of obedience, we cannot have peace within. When we read the book of Daniel, we understand that he and his three Israelite friends fasted against the king of Babylon's food and chose to eat only foods of the earth, which were plants. Their diet was all natural and nothing was processed, because they were choosing the way God intended for them to eat back home. They chose not to eat the food because they knew their bodies were temples of God and they did not want to ingest the tradition of the Babylonians; they chose to continue to follow God despite where they were.

When we fast, we are cleansing ourselves from the inside out, allowing our spirit to grow stronger so that it can withstand the trials of this world. Take Jesus, for instance: he fasted for forty days and forty nights in the wilderness, all as part of God's plan for him. He had to endure this because it was making him stronger so that he could bear the persecution ahead of him. He was taught how to beat the accuser with God's words and steady communication with God, who was giving him strength and understanding that when we are weak, he is strong; when our flesh weakens, God empowers our spirit and upholds us through all situations.

Fasting is a way of giving thanks to God for all his faithfulness. It helps our spirit grow and weakens our flesh; we think more clearly because we communicate with God and he maintains our strength and comfort through the fast. We must humbly fast to allow God to do what is needed for us; this is about the closeness between you and God. God will lead your direction in fasting. All you have to do is pray to him about what kind of fast he has for you and when he wants you to do it. Fasting is a part of our Christian walk. Many people before us have exemplified the reasoning and purpose and how it helps us conquer many trials that may come our way. Seek God in everything. Remember Matthew 4:4, which says man cannot live off bread alone, but by every word that comes from the mouth of God. God has promised to never leave, fail, or abandon us. His grace is sufficient enough, and his mercy is new upon us each and every day.

My Prayers to God in Times of the Valleys

Dear Heavenly Father,

I come to you with openness of heart, mind, body, and soul. I feel the waves of the waters coming toward me, the difficulties of the rivers, and the flames of the fire. I may feel this, but I know that you are with me. You are already preparing things in my favor behind the scenes. You have told me that you will never leave me helpless without support. You are my eternal rock. I place my all with you in the name of Jesus.

When I go through the troubled waters, you will be with me. When I go through the rivers of difficulties, I will not drown. When I go through the fire, it will not consume me. Even when doubt fills my mind, your comfort renews my hope and cheer. You are my strength and refuge; you hide me in the safety of your covenant from the hands of my enemies. I am more than a conqueror, more than victorious; I am an heir to your kingdom, and I will rejoice in you through it all.

No weapons formed against me shall prosper. I love you, Lord, with every part of me. Thank you for freeing me from the bondage and chains of this world because Jesus paid the price for me through his death. Nothing can separate your love from me.

I believe it and receive all that you have in store for me, in the name of Jesus Christ, my Messiah. I give thanks to my Lord and proclaim his greatness.

Jesus came to seek and safe all who are lost. I am a survivor through all things because more is with me than against me. I appreciate all you do for me and my family, children, friends, finances, health, marriage—just everything, Lord. I cannot do this life without you; you give me continuous joy through Christ. Amen, and glory be to God in the highest.

Masterpiece

When we think of a masterpiece, we see a magnificent creation that was made by an artist. That's how God sees us: as his divine masterpiece that he has taken time to create in his likeness. When the world tells you that you are worthless, you tell it that you are worth more than all the rubies in this world because you are being molded and processed by the king of all kings, our almighty God. The world sees the outward appearance of a person; however, God sees the heart of a person.

Many may look at a person and make prejudgment accusations, but God speaks within, telling you that you are a child of God and he will place you in front of all those who have done wrong to you, after his work is completed, through his son, Christ Jesus. We all must be patient as we are being processed, because perfection takes time.

Remember Genesis 1:27, "So God created human beings in his own image. In the image of God, he created them; male and female he created them." This is simply saying we are the children of God and are all masterpieces, no matter what the world may think of or say about us. Embrace the changes that our almighty God is doing in us all, through Christ.

Powerful Prayer to Defeat the Deception of the Devil

Father, God almighty, we come together to give thanks to you for all your faithfulness, greatness, and being so sovereign to us, in the name of Jesus. We humbly give to you all our worries and concerns, for we know that you will take care of all things. For your words say in 1 Peter 5:6, "So humble yourselves under the mighty power of God, and in due time he will lift you up in honor." We trust in, rely on, and have confident hope in you because we know that all things are possible with God. No matter what we may think about a situation, we know that you have promised to never leave, forsake, abandon, or fail us, for you are always a present help in times of trouble; you are our strength and refuge.

Keep us safe, O Lord God, from the loudness of this world; we are yours, and we belong to you, for you have foreordained us into your family through Christ. We believe in Christ, and we know that we as well as our household will be saved. We will place all our troubles at the foot of the cross because we know that by Christ's wounds we are healed from all the scars that the world has inflicted on us. We pray for your peace through Christ, our Lord and Savior.

Father, we rebuke, in the name of Jesus, all the torment, frustration, brokenness, and loss that the devil try to place upon us and our family. He's a liar and there is no truth in him. We serve a God who teaches us, through Christ, that we must focus on all the things up above, not these earthly things. All praises and worship given to God almighty, in Christ Jesus's name. Amen.

Morning Prayer

Thank you, Heavenly Father, for waking me up this morning. Thank you for having a watchful eye on me as I enter into the world. Your ears are constantly open to hear my prayers of appreciation and dedication to you in the name of Jesus. This day and every day will be great and joyous, for I have the king above all kings guiding and protecting me throughout the days, and your faithful promises are my armor and shield. I trust in you with all my heart, for you are my fortress and refuge. You protect me from dangers and you are my safety place in times of distress.

I will continuously give you thanks and proclaim your greatness, for your unfailing love endures forever. I will embrace every moment because you are with me wherever I go or stay, for you are my God. In Jesus's name, amen.

Good-Night Prayer

Father, thank you for this day that has ended. Continue to embrace me in your arms as I lie down and sleep. Be in control of my thoughts, so that I think only of your faithfulness, in Jesus's name.

I am covered with the blood of Christ as well as the angels to protect and guard me. I have no fears, for I know that you are with me. I sleep in peace because I am in the shelter of the Most High. No harm will come to me, my children, my family, and so on, because we are in your fortress, which protects us from all dangers. I freely give myself to you, for you to mold and prepare me in ways that only you can, through Christ.

I rest in total peace so that I can begin a new day in your covenant. I love you, Abba, and continue to thank you for every day and night, because you are the one who keeps us safe. Praises to you, in Jesus's name. Amen.

Letter from Me to God, the One Who Takes Care of Me Through It All

Dear Abba,

These last couple of days have been really trying as I acknowledge how your plans and ways for my life are always on time and on point. I must be honest: when unexpected things were happening, I began to get a little tart or frustrated. Then that small voice inside me was screaming, "Seek God through this. Do not let your thoughts or situation take you from him." I went back to my safe place in which the spirit within pointed me to Hebrews 13, where God says he will never leave or forsake us and will never leave us helpless without support. Then I was instructed to go to Isaiah 41, where God tells us, "Don't be afraid, for I am with you. Don't be discouraged, for I am your God."

Now, as I was listening to the scriptures, the spirit within was easing me from the inside out. I began to receive this unexplainable peace that came over me where it just seemed as though nothing could come against me. I felt like a superhero who had just received her powers to conquer the evil villains. All I could do is thank you, because you really do take care of all those who have faith in and rely on you. Even though my mind and emotions were beginning to boil over, you intercepted with Christ to pull me back to how your words never fail us; you are constantly watching over those who do good, fear you, and rely on your unfailing love.

I know your ears are open to my prayers, because as I was thanking and praising you, ideas of how to overcome the situation begin to become vivid. You reminded me how you give me resources in case of emergencies and that I must not put my faith in them, but in you. I was brought back to Matthew 6, where it says a person cannot serve two masters; he will hate one and love the other. Money is the root of all evil.

I serve you, Lord, and you will supply all that I need. A passage in that same book says to seek his kingdom and his righteousness, and all these things shall be given to you. Through this, you were showing me that no matter what I may see in front of me, you have the ultimate power to turn any situation around; all I must do is constantly seek you, through Christ.

Pray instead of becoming anxious or worrying, because that does nothing but cause other issues. I was told in Psalm 34 that many are the afflictions of the righteous, but the Lord rescues them each time.

Abba, I apologize for even having a moment of doubt, because you are constantly preparing and working behind the scenes to make all things new. You know all my weaknesses and are sharpening me through them all. I must accept the way that you do things and continue to focus on all your faithfulness, through Christ. I feel more peaceful through it all because I know that I am not alone. You, Christ, and the Holy Spirit are with me, fighting all my battles. I pray for continued peace, harmony, love, and humility in my family, children, marriage, decision making, and within. in Jesus's gracious name, amen.

Dear Heavenly Father

Thank you for your continued love and faithfulness, for being so sovereign to me, for your greatness, grace, favor, and mercy. You help me every moment of my life; I am forever grateful to you, in the name of Jesus Christ. I have no worries because I know and have faith and hope in you, Christ, and the Holy Spirit.

Thank you in advance for meeting all my needs (even my wants), restoring my marriage, my children, my family, my friends—everything, Lord. I send it all up to you in the name of Jesus Christ our Lord and Savior. Psalms 33:18 says, "But the Lord watches over those who fear him and rely on his unfailing love." I know that you are always watching over me, making sure that I follow the right path, through Christ. I am in the covenant of the Most High. Thanks again, Abba. Amen.

Printed in the United States
By Bookmasters